THE INTERNET OF THINGS IN AGRICULTURE

CONNECTING FARM EQUIPMENT AND FIELD DATA TO IMPROVE DECISION MAKING

VIPUL BAIBHAV

Made with ♥ on the Notion Press Platform
www.notionpress.com

"This book is dedicated to all the farmers who work tirelessly to feed the world. Their hard work and dedication to their craft inspire me to write about how technology can help them improve their yields and reduce their costs. May this book serve as a guide to help them navigate the ever-evolving landscape of agricultural technology."

And also to my family for their unwavering support and understanding during the time spent writing this book. Without their love and encouragement, this book would not have been possible.

And finally, to the future farmers and agricultural scientists, who will continue to shape the industry with their innovative ideas and advancements in technology. May this book inspire them to think creatively and push the boundaries of what is possible in agriculture.

Contents

Contents

FOREWORD

As the world's population continues to grow, the need for sustainable and efficient agricultural practices becomes increasingly important. The Internet of Things (IoT) offers a promising solution to these challenges, providing farmers with the tools they need to optimize crop yields and reduce costs.

In "The Internet of Things in Agriculture: Connecting Farm Equipment and Field Data to Improve Decision Making," author Vipul Baibav expertly guides readers through the intricacies of IoT in agriculture. From smart sensors and drones to precision agriculture and blockchain, Vipul covers all the latest developments in this rapidly advancing field.

Whether you are a farmer, agricultural scientist, or simply interested in the intersection of technology and agriculture, this book is an essential resource. It provides a comprehensive overview of the current state of IoT in agriculture and offers a glimpse into the future of this exciting field.

I highly recommend this book to anyone interested in the future of agriculture and the role that technology will play in shaping it.

Foreword by Vipul Baibhav

Preface

The agriculture industry is facing an increasing number of challenges as the world's population continues to grow. Climate change, water scarcity, and soil degradation are just a few of the problems that farmers are dealing with on a daily basis. The Internet of Things (IoT) offers a way to address these challenges by providing farmers with the tools they need to optimize crop yields and reduce costs.

In this book, "The Internet of Things in Agriculture: Connecting Farm Equipment and Field Data to Improve Decision Making," I delve into the various aspects of IoT in agriculture. From smart sensors and drones to precision agriculture and blockchain, I cover the latest developments in this rapidly advancing field. I also discuss the challenges and limitations of using IoT in agriculture, as well as the potential benefits for farmers, agricultural scientists, and the industry as a whole.

This book is not just for farmers or agricultural scientists, but for anyone interested in the intersection of technology and agriculture. I hope that this book will serve as a guide for those looking to understand the current state of IoT in agriculture and its potential for the future.

I would like to thank everyone who supported me during the writing of this book, especially my family and friends for their patience and understanding. I would also like to thank the experts and researchers in the field who shared their insights and knowledge with me.

ACKNOWLEDGEMENTS

First and foremost, I would like to thank my family for their unwavering support and understanding during the time spent writing this book. Their love and encouragement kept me going, and I couldn't have done it without them.

I would also like to thank the experts and researchers in the field of IoT in agriculture who shared their insights and knowledge with me. Their contributions have been invaluable in helping me to understand the complexities of this rapidly evolving field.

I would also like to extend my gratitude to my editors and publishers, who helped to shape and refine the book, and provided valuable feedback and suggestions.

Lastly, I would like to thank all the farmers, who work tirelessly to feed the world. Their hard work and dedication to their craft inspired me to write this book, and I hope that it will serve as a guide to help them navigate the ever-evolving landscape of agricultural technology.

Thank you all for your support, and I hope you enjoy reading this book as much as I enjoyed writing it.

Sincerely,

Vipul Baibhav

Author of "The Internet of Things in Agriculture: Connecting Farm Equipment and Field Data to Improve Decision Making"

PROLOGUE

The world is changing at a rapid pace, and agriculture is no exception. As the global population continues to grow, the demand for food is increasing, and farmers are facing an increasing number of challenges. Climate change, water scarcity, and soil degradation are just a few of the problems that farmers are dealing with on a daily basis.

In this book, "The Internet of Things in Agriculture: Connecting Farm Equipment and Field Data to Improve Decision Making," we will explore how the Internet of Things (IoT) can be used to address these challenges and provide farmers with the tools they need to optimize crop yields and reduce costs.

From smart sensors and drones to precision agriculture and blockchain, we will cover the latest developments in this rapidly advancing field. We will also discuss the challenges and limitations of using IoT in agriculture, as well as the potential benefits for farmers, agricultural scientists, and the industry as a whole.

This book is not just for farmers or agricultural scientists, but for anyone interested in the intersection of technology and agriculture. Our goal is to provide a comprehensive and accessible overview of the current state of IoT in agriculture and its potential for the future.

So, whether you are a farmer looking to improve your yields or a student interested in the future of agriculture, this book is for you. Join us as we explore the exciting world of IoT in agriculture.

Prologue by Vipul Baibhav

I

Introduction

The Internet of Things (IoT) is transforming the way we live, work, and play. It is also transforming the way we farm. IoT in agriculture refers to the use of connected devices and sensors to gather data on crop and soil conditions, weather, and livestock health. This data is then analyzed to optimize crop yields and reduce costs, as well as to improve decision making on the farm.

In this book, "The Internet of Things in Agriculture: Connecting Farm Equipment and Field Data to Improve Decision Making," we will take a closer look at how IoT is being used in agriculture today and how it has the potential to shape the future of farming. We will explore the various devices and sensors that are being used in agriculture, such as smart sensors for measuring soil moisture and temperature, drones for crop scouting and monitoring, and weather stations for collecting weather data. We will also examine the platforms and tools used to collect, store, and analyze IoT data and how this data can be used to optimize crop yields and reduce costs.

We will also delve into the topic of precision agriculture and how IoT is being used to improve precision agriculture. We will explore the use of IoT data to improve crop management and increase crop yields. We will also discuss IoT and Livestock Management and how IoT data can be used to improve livestock health and reduce costs.

In addition, we will cover the challenges and limitations of using IoT in agriculture, such as privacy and security concerns, and the need for reliable internet connectivity in rural areas. We will also discuss the potential benefits of using IoT in agriculture, such as traceability and transparency in food supply chains.

This book is aimed at farmers, agricultural scientists, and anyone interested in the intersection of technology and agriculture. Whether you're looking to improve your yields or simply want to understand the current state of IoT in agriculture, this book is for you.

Overview of IoT in agriculture

The Internet of Things (IoT) in agriculture refers to the use of connected devices and sensors to gather data on crop and soil conditions, weather, and livestock health. This data is then analyzed to optimize crop yields and reduce costs, as well as to improve decision making on the farm.

IoT devices and sensors used in agriculture include:

- Smart sensors for measuring soil moisture, temperature, and nutrient levels
- Drones for crop scouting and monitoring
- Weather stations for collecting weather data
- Livestock monitoring devices for tracking animal health and behavior
- Automated irrigation and fertilization systems
- Soil pH, EC and temperature sensors

The data collected by these devices is transmitted to the cloud, where it can be analyzed using big data and machine learning algorithms. The data can be used to optimize irrigation, fertilization, and pest management, as well as to monitor crop and livestock health.

IoT in agriculture also has the potential to improve traceability and transparency in food supply chains. Blockchain technology can be used to create a secure and tamper-proof record of the food product journey from farm to consumer, which can improve food safety and reduce food waste.

Precision agriculture is one of the main applications of IoT in agriculture, it allows farmers to optimize crop management by using real-time data to make informed decisions. For example, using IoT data, farmers can adjust the amount of water and fertilizer they use based on the specific needs of their crops, which can lead to increased yields and reduced costs.

However, there are also challenges and limitations to using IoT in agriculture, such as privacy and security concerns, and the need for reliable internet connectivity in rural areas. In addition, the cost of IoT devices and sensors can be a barrier to adoption,

especially for small farmers. Another challenge is the integration and compatibility of different devices and platforms, as well as the need for skilled personnel to manage and analyze the data.

Despite these challenges, the potential benefits of IoT in agriculture are significant, and the industry is expected to continue to grow in the coming years. Many companies and organizations are investing in IoT-based agricultural solutions, and farmers are starting to adopt these technologies at a faster rate.

In conclusion, IoT in agriculture has the potential to revolutionize the way we farm, making it more sustainable, efficient, and profitable. By connecting farm equipment and field data, farmers can make better-informed decisions and optimize their operations to improve crop yields and reduce costs. As the technology continues to evolve, we can expect to see even more advancements in the field of IoT in agriculture in the future.

Benefits of IoT for farmers and the agricultural industry

The Internet of Things (IoT) in agriculture offers a wide range of benefits for farmers and the agricultural industry as a whole. Some of these benefits include:

1. Increased crop yields: IoT devices and sensors can be used to gather data on crop and soil conditions, weather, and pests. This data can be analyzed to optimize irrigation, fertilization, and pest management, leading to increased crop yields and reduced costs.
2. Precision agriculture: IoT data can be used to improve precision agriculture by providing farmers with real-time information on crop and soil conditions. This allows them to make informed decisions on when to plant, water, and harvest their crops, leading to increased yields and reduced costs.
3. Livestock management: IoT devices and sensors can be used to monitor and track the health and behavior of livestock. This data can be used to improve feed management, detect illnesses, and reduce costs associated with animal care.
4. Traceability and transparency: IoT can be used to create a secure and tamper-proof record of the food product journey from farm to consumer. This can improve food safety and reduce food waste.

5. Efficiency: IoT technology can automate many tasks on the farm, such as irrigation and fertilization, reducing the need for human labor and increasing efficiency.
6. Cost savings: IoT technology can help farmers reduce costs associated with irrigation, fertilization, pest management, and animal care.
7. Environmental benefits: IoT technology can be used to monitor and reduce water and energy consumption on the farm, leading to environmental benefits such as water conservation and reduced carbon footprint.
8. Better decision making: IoT data can be used to provide farmers with
9. real-time information on crop and soil conditions, weather, and livestock health, allowing them to make better-informed decisions. This can improve the overall productivity and profitability of the farm.
10. Remote monitoring: IoT technology allows farmers to remotely monitor and control their equipment and crops, even when they are away from the farm, which can help them save time and money.
11. Predictive maintenance: IoT devices and sensors can be used to predict when equipment needs maintenance, reducing downtime and increasing productivity.

These are just some of the many benefits that IoT can offer for farmers and the agricultural industry. As technology continues to evolve and more devices and sensors become available, we can expect to see even more advancements in the field of IoT in agriculture in the future.

II

IoT Devices and Sensors in Agriculture

There are a wide variety of IoT devices and sensors that can be used in agriculture, each with its own specific function. Some of the most common IoT devices and sensors in agriculture include:

- Smart sensors: These sensors can be used to measure soil moisture, temperature, and nutrient levels, as well as to detect pests and diseases. Some examples include soil moisture sensors, temperature sensors, and pH sensors.
- Drones: Drones can be used for crop scouting, monitoring crop growth, and identifying pests and diseases. They can also be used for mapping and surveying land.

- Weather stations: These devices can be used to collect data on weather conditions, such as temperature, humidity, wind speed, and rainfall. This data can be used to optimize irrigation and fertilization.
- Livestock monitoring devices: These devices can be used to track the health and behavior of livestock, such as heart rate, temperature, and movement.
- Automated irrigation and fertilization systems: These systems can be controlled and monitored remotely, using data from weather stations and soil sensors to optimize irrigation and fertilization.
- Smart cameras and image recognition software: These devices can be used to identify pests and diseases, and to monitor crop growth and health.
- GPS and mapping technology: This technology can be used for mapping and surveying land, as well as for precision agriculture and crop management.
- Biometric sensors for Livestock: These sensors can monitor the vital signs of livestock such as heart rate, respiration, temperature, and activity levels.

These are just a few examples of the many IoT devices and sensors that can be used in agriculture. As technology continues to evolve, we can expect to see even more advancements in this field in the future.

Overview of different types of IoT devices and sensors used in agriculture

In agriculture, IoT devices and sensors are used to collect data on various aspects of crop growth and soil conditions. These devices can be grouped into several categories:

- Weather sensors: These devices measure temperature, humidity, precipitation, wind speed and direction, and solar radiation. This information is used to optimize irrigation and crop management.
- Soil sensors: These devices measure soil moisture, pH, nutrient levels, and temperature. This information is used to optimize irrigation and fertilization.
- Crop sensors: These devices measure crop growth, including plant height, leaf area, and fruit yield. This information is used to optimize crop management and harvest timing.
- Livestock sensors: These devices monitor the health and activity of livestock, including temperature, heart rate, and movement.
- Unmanned aerial vehicles (UAVs) and drones: These devices are used to collect data on crop growth and soil conditions, as well as to spray crops with fertilizers or pesticides.

- Smart greenhouses: These are IoT-enabled greenhouses that use sensors, automated systems, and data analysis to optimize crop growth and energy efficiency.
- Automated irrigation systems: These systems use sensors to measure soil moisture and weather data to automatically adjust irrigation schedules.
- Livestock monitoring systems: These systems use sensors and cameras to monitor the health and well-being of livestock, including feed and water intake, and movement.

These are some of the common IoT devices and sensors used in agriculture, but there are many other applications and devices that are being developed.

Examples of IoT devices that can be used in agriculture

Here are some examples of IoT devices that can be used in agriculture:

1. Weather stations: These devices measure temperature, humidity, precipitation, wind speed, and direction, and solar radiation. They can be used to optimize irrigation and crop management.
2. Soil moisture sensors: These devices measure the water content of soil and can be used to optimize irrigation schedules.
3. Crop sensors: These devices use cameras and machine learning algorithms to monitor crop growth and predict yields.
4. Livestock monitoring systems: These devices use sensors to monitor the health and activity of livestock, including temperature, heart rate, and movement.
5. Unmanned aerial vehicles (UAVs) and drones: These devices can be used to collect data on crop growth and soil conditions, as well as to spray crops with fertilizers or pesticides.
6. Smart greenhouses: These are IoT-enabled greenhouses that use sensors, automated systems, and data analysis to optimize crop growth and energy efficiency.
7. Automated irrigation systems: These systems use sensors to measure soil moisture and weather data to automatically adjust irrigation schedules.

8. Livestock monitoring systems: These systems use sensors and cameras to monitor the health and well-being of livestock, including feed and water intake, and movement.
9. Wireless sensor networks: These networks consist of multiple sensor nodes that can be placed in the field to collect data on weather, soil, and crop conditions.
10. Precision farming systems: These are systems that use data from IoT devices and sensors to optimize farming operations, including planting, fertilization, and harvesting.

These are just a few examples of IoT devices that can be used in agriculture. As technology continues to advance, new IoT devices and sensors are being developed to help farmers make more informed decisions and improve crop yields.

Discussion of the benefits of using IoT devices in agriculture

IoT (Internet of Things) applications can benefit agriculture in several ways, such as:

- Precision agriculture: IoT devices can be used to monitor soil moisture, temperature, and other environmental factors to optimize crop growth and reduce waste.
- Livestock monitoring: IoT devices can be used to monitor the health and well-being of livestock, such as by monitoring their movement and activity levels.
- Equipment tracking: IoT devices can be used to track and monitor agricultural equipment, such as tractors and harvesters, to improve efficiency and reduce downtime.
- Pest and disease management: IoT devices can be used to detect and track pests and diseases in crops, allowing for early intervention and reducing the need for chemical pesticides.
- Weather monitoring: IoT devices can be used to monitor weather patterns and forecast weather, which can help farmers make more informed decisions about planting and harvesting.

Overall, IoT can help farmers make more data-driven decisions and be more efficient in their operations.

III

Connecting and Analyzing IoT Data

Connecting and analyzing IoT data involves several steps:

- Data collection: IoT devices, such as sensors and cameras, collect data from the field. This data is then sent to a central location, such as a cloud server or a local gateway, for processing.
- Data transmission: The collected data is then transmitted to a central location, such as a cloud server or a local gateway, for processing. This can be done through wired or wireless networks, such as Wi-Fi or cellular networks.
- Data storage: The collected data is then stored in a database for future analysis. This can be done in the cloud or on-premises, depending on the specific application.
- Data processing: The collected data is then processed to extract useful information. This can be done using

various techniques such as machine learning, statistical analysis, and data visualization.

- Data analysis: The processed data is then analyzed to gain insights and make decisions. This can be done using various tools such as dashboards, reports, and alerts.
- Data action: The insights gained from the data analysis are then used to take action such as adjusting irrigation systems or activating alarms.

Overall, the process of connecting and analyzing IoT data involves collecting data from IoT devices, transmitting it to a central location, storing it, processing it, analyzing it, and taking action based on the insights gained.

Tools used to collect, store, and analyze IoT data

There are several tools that can be used to collect, store, and analyze IoT data, such as:

- Data collection tools: IoT devices, such as sensors and cameras, are used to collect data from the field. These devices can be connected to a central location, such as a cloud server or a local gateway, through wired or wireless networks, such as Wi-Fi or cellular networks.
- Data storage tools: Cloud databases such as AWS IoT, Azure IoT and Google Cloud IoT are used to store the collected data for future analysis. NoSQL databases like MongoDB and Cassandra are also used for storing IoT data.
- Data processing tools: Apache Kafka, Apache Storm, and Apache Spark can be used to process the collected data in real-time. They are used to extract useful information and perform data cleansing, data transformation, and data integration.
- Data analysis tools: Tools like Tableau, Power BI, and Looker are used to visualize the data and extract insights. Machine learning platforms like Tensorflow, Pytorch, scikit-learn and cloud-based machine learning platforms like AWS SageMaker, Azure Machine Learning, and Google Cloud ML Engine are used to analyze the data and make predictions.

- Data action tools: Platforms like AWS IoT, Azure IoT, and Google Cloud IoT can be used to take action based on the insights gained from the data analysis.

Overall, the tools used to collect, store, and analyze IoT data vary depending on the specific application, but they typically involve a combination of IoT devices, data storage and processing tools, data analysis tools, and data action platforms.

How IoT data can be used to optimize crop yields and reduce costs

IoT (Internet of Things) data can be used to optimize crop yields and reduce costs in several ways:

- Smart irrigation: IoT sensors can be used to monitor soil moisture levels and adjust irrigation systems accordingly, reducing water waste and increasing crop yields.
- Precision agriculture: IoT devices can be used to gather data on weather conditions, soil moisture, and crop growth, which can be used to optimize planting, fertilization, and harvesting times, increasing crop yields and reducing costs.
- Pest and disease management: IoT sensors can be used to monitor crop health and detect pests or diseases early, allowing farmers to take action before they cause significant damage.
- Livestock management: IoT devices can be used to monitor the health and well-being of livestock, such as cows, pigs, and chickens, and take action to improve their well-being, increase milk production, and reduce costs.
- Smart greenhouses: IoT sensors can be used to monitor temperature, humidity, and light levels in greenhouses,

allowing farmers to optimize growing conditions and increase crop yields.

Overall, IoT data can be used to optimize crop yields and reduce costs by providing farmers with real-time data and insights on crop and livestock health, weather conditions, and other factors that affect their operations.

How IoT data is used to optimize irrigation, fertilization, and pest management

IoT data can be used to optimize irrigation, fertilization, and pest management in several ways:

- Smart irrigation: IoT sensors can be used to monitor soil moisture levels and adjust irrigation systems accordingly, reducing water waste and increasing crop yields. For example, sensors can measure the soil moisture and can trigger the irrigation system to turn on when the moisture level falls below a certain threshold.
- Precision agriculture: IoT devices can be used to gather data on weather conditions, soil moisture, and crop growth, which can be used to optimize planting, fertilization, and harvesting times, increasing crop yields and reducing costs. The data can also be used to adjust the type and amount of fertilizer applied, based on the specific needs of the crop.
- Pest and disease management: IoT sensors can be used to monitor crop health and detect pests or diseases early, allowing farmers to take action before they cause significant damage. The data can also be used to

identify the specific pests or diseases present, and to choose the most appropriate treatment.

- Livestock management: IoT devices can be used to monitor the health and well-being of livestock, such as cows, pigs, and chickens, and take action to improve their well-being, increase milk production, and reduce costs. For example, sensors can monitor cow's health, and can alert farmers if a cow is showing signs of illness.

Overall, IoT data can be used to optimize irrigation, fertilization, and pest management by providing farmers with real-time data and insights on crop and livestock health, weather conditions, and other factors that affect their operations, allowing them to make data-driven decisions and improve their crop yields and reduce costs.

IV

IoT and Precision Agriculture

Precision agriculture is the use of advanced technology, such as IoT devices, to gather and analyze data on weather conditions, soil moisture, crop growth, and other factors, in order to optimize planting, fertilization, and harvesting times. By using IoT devices, farmers can collect and analyze large amounts of data in real-time, which can help them make more informed decisions about their operations.

IoT devices such as sensors, drones, and cameras can be used to gather data on various aspects of farming operations, such as soil moisture, weather conditions, crop growth, and pest and disease management. This data can be used to optimize irrigation systems, adjust fertilizer application rates, identify pests and diseases early, and make other data-driven decisions that can improve crop yields and reduce costs.

For example, IoT sensors can be used to monitor soil moisture levels and trigger irrigation systems to turn on when the moisture level falls below a certain threshold. Drones can be used to gather data on crop growth and health, and cameras can be used to monitor crop development, detect pests and diseases, and identify areas of the field that may need attention.

In addition, IoT devices can also be used to control and automate farming equipment, such as tractors and harvesting machines, which can improve efficiency and reduce costs.

Overall, IoT and precision agriculture can help farmers make data-driven decisions that can improve crop yields and reduce costs by providing real-time data and insights on weather conditions, soil moisture, crop growth, and other factors that affect their operations.

Overview of precision agriculture

Precision agriculture is a farming management approach that uses advanced technology to optimize crop yields and reduce costs. This approach is characterized by the use of data collection and analysis, GPS technology, and automation to improve decision-making and management practices throughout the growing season.

The goal of precision agriculture is to optimize crop yields by using technology to gather and analyze data on weather conditions, soil moisture, crop growth, and other factors that can affect crop health and yield. This data is then used to make more informed decisions about planting, fertilization, irrigation, and pest management.

Some key components of precision agriculture include:

1. IoT devices such as sensors, drones, and cameras to gather data on weather conditions, soil moisture, crop growth, and pest management.
2. GPS technology to map fields, track equipment, and guide planting and harvesting.
3. Automation of farming equipment such as tractors and harvesters to improve efficiency and reduce costs.
4. Software and platforms that integrate data from various sources and provide insights to farmers.

5. Remote sensing and image processing technology to monitor crop growth and health from the air or from satellites

Precision agriculture can provide farmers with a more accurate understanding of the conditions of their field, allowing them to make better decisions about planting, fertilization, irrigation and pest management. This can result in improved crop yields and reduced costs. Additionally, precision agriculture can also help farmers to identify problem areas, such as pests or diseases, early, which can prevent significant damage and save on treatment costs.

How IoT is used to improve precision agriculture

IoT (Internet of Things) technology can be used to improve precision agriculture by providing farmers with real-time data and insights on weather conditions, soil moisture, crop growth, and other factors that affect their operations. This allows farmers to make more informed decisions about planting, fertilization, irrigation, and pest management, which can improve crop yields and reduce costs.

Some specific ways in which IoT can be used to improve precision agriculture include:

Smart sensors: IoT sensors can be placed in the field to gather data on soil moisture, temperature, and other factors that affect crop growth. This data can be used to optimize irrigation systems, adjust fertilizer application rates, and make other data-driven decisions that can improve crop yields and reduce costs.

Drones: IoT-enabled drones can be used to gather data on crop growth and health, including leaf area index, plant height, and canopy cover. This data can be used to identify problem areas, such as pests or diseases, early, which can prevent significant damage and save on treatment costs.

Smart cameras: IoT-enabled cameras can be used to monitor crop development, detect pests and diseases, and identify areas of the field that may need attention. This data can be used to optimize planting, fertilization, and harvesting times, and improve crop yields.

Automation: IoT-enabled farming equipment, such as tractors and harvesters, can be controlled and automated using data gathered from sensors and cameras, improving efficiency and reducing costs.

Software and platforms: IoT data can be integrated into software and platforms that provide farmers with insights on weather conditions, soil moisture, crop growth, and other factors that affect their operations. This allows farmers to make more informed decisions about planting, fertilization, irrigation, and pest management.

Overall, IoT technology can be used to improve precision agriculture by providing farmers with real-time data and insights that can be used to optimize planting, fertilization, irrigation, and pest management, which can improve crop yields and reduce costs.

How IoT data can be used to improve crop management

IoT data can be used to improve crop management in several ways. By using sensors placed in fields, farmers can collect data on soil moisture, temperature, and nutrient levels, which can be used to optimize irrigation and fertilization. Additionally, IoT devices such as weather stations and drones can be used to gather data on weather patterns and crop growth, which can help farmers make more informed decisions about planting, harvesting, and pest control. This data can also be used to create predictive models that can help farmers anticipate issues and take preventative measures. Additionally, IoT devices can also be used to track the location and health of livestock, which can improve the efficiency of animal husbandry.

Examples of precision agriculture applications using IoT data

1. Field mapping and monitoring: IoT sensors can be used to collect data on factors such as soil moisture, temperature, and nutrient levels, which can then be used to create detailed maps of field conditions. This information can be used to optimize crop yields, identify areas that may be at risk of disease or pests, and plan irrigation and fertilization schedules.
2. Crop monitoring: IoT-enabled cameras and sensors can be used to monitor crop growth, health, and yield in real-time. This information can be used to detect early signs of stress or disease, which can help farmers take action before significant damage is done.
3. Livestock monitoring: IoT devices can be used to monitor the health and well-being of livestock. This includes monitoring factors such as temperature, activity levels, and feeding patterns. This information can be used to optimize animal health and productivity, and to identify and address potential issues early on.
4. Autonomous vehicles and drones: IoT-enabled autonomous vehicles and drones can be used to perform tasks such as planting, harvesting, and spraying crops. These vehicles can be programmed to

follow precise routes and perform specific tasks, which can help optimize efficiency and reduce labor costs.

5. Weather forecasting: IoT devices can be used to collect data on weather patterns and conditions, which can be used to create detailed weather forecasts. This information can help farmers plan their operations, such as when to plant, fertilize, and harvest their crops, and can help avoid crop damage due to extreme weather events.

V

IoT and Livestock Management

IoT technology can be used in a variety of ways to improve livestock management. Some examples include:

1. Livestock tracking: IoT devices, such as RFID tags, can be used to track the location, movement, and behavior of individual animals. This information can be used to optimize herd health and productivity, and to identify and address potential issues early on.
2. Health monitoring: IoT-enabled sensors can be used to monitor the health and well-being of individual animals. This includes monitoring factors such as temperature, activity levels, and feeding patterns. This information can be used to detect early signs of illness or injury, which can help farmers take action before significant damage is done.
3. Feed management: IoT devices can be used to monitor and manage feed intake, which can help optimize

animal health and productivity. This includes monitoring factors such as feed consumption, digestion, and nutrient absorption.

4. Climate control: IoT-enabled sensors and devices can be used to monitor and control the environment in which livestock are kept. This includes monitoring factors such as temperature, humidity, and ventilation, which can help maintain optimal living conditions for the animals.
5. Automated milking: IoT technology can be used to automate the milking process for dairy cattle, which can help increase efficiency and reduce labor costs. This includes systems that automatically detect when a cow is ready to be milked and then complete the milking process without human intervention.

Overview of IoT devices and sensors used in livestock management

There are a variety of IoT devices and sensors that can be used in livestock management, here are some examples:

- RFID tags: RFID tags are small, wireless devices that can be attached to animals. They can be used to track the location, movement, and behavior of individual animals, which can help optimize herd health and productivity, and identify and address potential issues early on.
- Biometric sensors: These sensors can be used to monitor the health and well-being of individual animals. Examples include sensors that monitor temperature, activity levels, and heart rate. This information can be used to detect early signs of illness or injury, which can help farmers take action before significant damage is done.
- Feed intake sensors: These sensors can be used to monitor and manage feed intake. They can measure the amount of feed consumed by an animal, and can provide information on digestion and nutrient absorption.
- Environmental sensors: These sensors can be used to monitor and control the environment in which

livestock are kept. Examples include sensors that monitor temperature, humidity, and ventilation. This information can be used to maintain optimal living conditions for the animals.

- Automated milking systems: These systems can be used to automate the milking process for dairy cattle. They use sensors to detect when a cow is ready to be milked and then complete the milking process without human intervention.
- Camera: IoT enabled cameras can be used to monitor the overall health and behavior of the livestock, and can detect early signs of stress or disease, which can help farmers take action before significant damage is done.
- GPS: GPS trackers can be used to monitor the location and movements of individual animals, which can be useful in tracking the animals in large pastures or during transport.

How IoT data can be used to improve livestock health and reduce costs

IoT data can be used to improve livestock health and reduce costs in a number of ways:

- Early detection of illness or injury: IoT sensors can be used to monitor the health and well-being of individual animals in real-time. This information can be used to detect early signs of illness or injury, which can help farmers take action before significant damage is done. Early detection can reduce the spread of disease, and can help prevent costly treatments and losses.
- Optimizing herd health: IoT data can be used to create detailed profiles of individual animals, which can help farmers identify and address potential issues early on. This includes monitoring factors such as temperature, activity levels, and feeding patterns. This information can be used to optimize herd health and productivity.
- Automating feeding and management: IoT-enabled devices can be used to monitor and manage feed intake, which can help optimize animal health and productivity. This includes systems that automatically dispense feed and monitor consumption. Automation can help reduce labor costs and increase efficiency.

- Improving climate control: IoT-enabled sensors and devices can be used to monitor and control the environment in which livestock are kept. This includes monitoring factors such as temperature, humidity, and ventilation. This information can be used to maintain optimal living conditions for the animals, which can improve their health and productivity.
- Predictive maintenance: IoT data can be used to predict when equipment or infrastructure such as barns, fences, etc. need maintenance. This allows farmers to schedule and plan maintenance, reducing downtime and costs.
- Livestock tracking: IoT data can be used to track the location and movements of individual animals, which can help farmers monitor the overall health and well-being of their herd, which can improve efficiency and reduce costs.
- Automated milking: IoT technology can be used to automate the milking process for dairy cattle, which can help increase efficiency and reduce labor costs.

Overall, the use of IoT technology in livestock management can help farmers make more informed decisions, improve herd health, and reduce costs.

IoT-based systems for monitoring livestock health, feed consumption, and movement

There are several IoT-based systems that can be used for monitoring livestock health, feed consumption, and movement:

- Livestock health monitoring systems: These systems use sensors and devices to monitor the health and well-being of individual animals in real-time. This includes monitoring factors such as temperature, activity levels, and heart rate. The data can be used to detect early signs of illness or injury, and can be integrated with other systems to optimize herd health and productivity.
- Feed intake monitoring systems: These systems use sensors and devices to monitor and manage feed intake. They can measure the amount of feed consumed by an animal, and can provide information on digestion and nutrient absorption. This information can be used to optimize feed management and improve animal health.
- Livestock tracking systems: These systems use RFID tags, GPS, or other tracking devices to monitor the

location and movements of individual animals. This information can be used to optimize herd management and monitor the overall health and well-being of the herd.

- Automated feeding systems: These systems use IoT-enabled devices to automatically dispense feed, monitor consumption, and adjust feed schedules based on animal needs. These systems can help optimize feed management, reduce labor costs and increase efficiency.
- Automated milking systems: These systems use IoT-enabled sensors to detect when a cow is ready to be milked and then complete the milking process without human intervention. This can help increase efficiency and reduce labor costs.
- Environmental monitoring systems: These systems use IoT-enabled sensors to monitor and control the environment in which livestock are kept. This includes monitoring factors such as temperature, humidity, and ventilation. This information can be used to maintain optimal living conditions for the animals, which can improve their health and productivity.

All these systems can be integrated with a central platform where farmers can access, analyze, and act on the data collected.

VI

Challenges and Limitations

While IoT-based systems for monitoring livestock health, feed consumption, and movement have many potential benefits, there are also some challenges and limitations to consider:

- Cost: Implementing IoT-based systems for monitoring livestock can be expensive. The cost of purchasing and installing sensors and devices, as well as the cost of maintaining and upgrading the systems, can be significant.
- Data management: Collecting and analyzing large amounts of data from IoT sensors can be challenging. It requires a robust and secure system for data storage, processing, and analysis.
- Network infrastructure: In order for IoT-based systems to function properly, a reliable and robust network infrastructure is required. This includes internet

connectivity, as well as the necessary hardware and software to support the systems.

- Power supply: In some cases, providing power to the IoT devices and sensors can be a challenge, particularly in remote locations. This can be overcome by using solar panels or batteries, but it can add to the cost of the system.
- Complexity: Some IoT-based systems can be complex to set up and maintain, and may require specialized skills and knowledge. This can make it difficult for farmers to fully utilize the systems.
- Interoperability: IoT devices and systems often use different communication protocols, making it difficult for devices from different vendors to communicate with one another.
- Security: IoT systems can be vulnerable to cyber-attacks, and it is important to have proper security measures in place to protect the systems and the data they collect.
- Animal welfare: Some IoT devices and systems can be invasive or uncomfortable for animals. It is important to ensure that the use of these systems does not compromise the welfare of the animals.

Overall, while IoT-based systems for monitoring livestock health, feed consumption, and movement have many potential benefits, it is important to carefully consider the challenges and limitations before implementing them.

Privacy and security concerns related to IoT in agriculture

There are several privacy and security concerns related to the use of IoT in agriculture, including:

- Data privacy: IoT systems collect a large amount of data, which could be sensitive and personal. This includes information about individual farmers, their land, crops, and livestock. It is important to ensure that data privacy is maintained and that data is not shared without proper consent.
- Cybersecurity: IoT systems are vulnerable to cyber-attacks, such as hacking, data breaches, and malware. This can expose sensitive data and lead to significant financial losses. It is important to have robust security measures in place to protect the systems and the data they collect.
- Access control: IoT systems need to be protected from unauthorized access, to ensure that only authorized personnel can access the data and control the systems. This includes implementing measures such as secure login, password protection, and encryption.
- Device security: IoT devices and sensors are vulnerable to physical tampering or hacking. This includes measures like firmware updates, adding physical

protection to devices and implementing secure boot procedures.

- Data ownership: There are concerns about who owns the data generated by IoT systems, and how it can be used. It is important to have clear agreements in place to ensure that farmers retain ownership of their data, and that it is used ethically and responsibly.
- Compliance: IoT systems in agriculture are subject to various regulations, such as data protection laws, and farmers need to be aware of the compliance requirements and ensure their systems comply with them.

Overall, privacy and security are critical issues when implementing IoT systems in agriculture. It is important to have robust security measures in place to protect the systems and the data they collect, while also ensuring data privacy and compliance with the regulations.

VII

How to overcome these challenges and limitations

There are several ways to overcome the challenges and limitations of using IoT in agriculture:

- Cost: To overcome the cost challenge, farmers can explore cost-effective solutions such as open-source hardware and software, and can also look into government grants and subsidies to help offset the costs.
- Data management: To overcome data management challenges, farmers can invest in robust and secure data management systems, and can also consider working with third-party providers who specialize in data management and analysis.
- Network infrastructure: To overcome network infrastructure challenges, farmers can invest in wireless technologies such as LoRaWAN, Sigfox, or LTE-M which

can provide low-cost and low-power connectivity even in remote areas.

- Power supply: To overcome power supply challenges, farmers can use solar panels or batteries to power IoT devices and sensors.
- Complexity: To overcome complexity challenges, farmers can work with technology providers who specialize in IoT solutions for agriculture and can provide training and support to help farmers fully utilize the systems.
- Interoperability: To overcome interoperability challenges, farmers can work with technology providers who specialize in IoT solutions for agriculture, and can ensure that devices and systems are able to communicate with one another.
- Security: To overcome security challenges, farmers can invest in robust security measures such as encryption, secure login, and password protection, and can work with security experts to identify and mitigate potential threats.
- Privacy: To overcome privacy challenges, farmers can implement data security measures like encryption, data anonymization, and user authentication to protect their data. They can also consider using a data governance framework to manage their data and ensure compliance with regulations.
- Weather conditions: To overcome the weather conditions challenges, farmers can use technologies like satellite connectivity, which are less affected by weather conditions.
- Integration: To overcome integration challenges, farmers can work with technology providers that can integrate IoT systems with existing systems, and can

provide training and support to help farmers fully utilize the systems.

Overall, it's important for farmers to take a holistic approach when implementing IoT systems in agriculture, considering cost, data management, network infrastructure, power supply, complexity, interoperability, security, privacy, weather conditions, and integration.

VIII

Summary of the benefits of using IoT in agriculture

IoT technology in agriculture can bring several benefits, including:

Increased efficiency and productivity: IoT-based systems can provide farmers with detailed data and insights that can be used to optimize crop yields, improve herd health, and reduce costs.

Real-time monitoring: IoT sensors and devices can be used to monitor crops, soil conditions, weather patterns, and livestock in real-time, which can help farmers make more informed decisions.

Automation: IoT-based systems can be used to automate tasks such as planting, harvesting, and feeding, which can help reduce labor costs and increase efficiency.

Predictive maintenance: IoT data can be used to predict when equipment or infrastructure needs maintenance, reducing downtime and costs.

Climate control: IoT-enabled sensors and devices can be used to monitor and control the environment in which crops and livestock are kept, which can help maintain optimal living conditions for the animals.

Livestock tracking: IoT data can be used to track the location and movements of individual animals, which can help farmers monitor the overall health and well-being of their herd, which can improve efficiency and reduce costs.

Weather forecasting: IoT devices can be used to collect data on weather patterns and conditions, which can be used to create detailed weather forecasts. This information can help farmers plan their operations, such as when to plant, fertilize, and harvest their crops, and can help avoid crop damage due to extreme weather events.

Overall, the use of IoT technology in agriculture can help farmers make more informed decisions, improve crop and livestock yields, reduce costs, and increase efficiency and productivity. The technology can also help farmers to be more aware of the weather patterns and conditions, and take action to prevent crop damage from extreme weather events. Additionally, the technology can help farmers to predict the maintenance of their equipment and infrastructure, reducing downtime and costs. With the real-time monitoring feature that IoT technology provides, farmers can have a greater understanding of their land, crops, and livestock, and make better decisions to improve their operations.

IX

Future outlook for IoT in agriculture

The use cases for IoT in agriculture are vast, and the list is continuously growing. Here are some examples:

- Precision farming — This is the aforementioned growth-driver for the industry, as well as a high-demand practice. Changing weather patterns and diminishing resources are raising an urgent need for optimizing crop production. Through the use of IoT devices that provide remote sensing, guidance, sensors, yield monitors, field mapping, and much more, precision farming is made possible.
- Crop management — Networked sensors can automate field processes and crop management by providing dynamic, relevant, real time information to farmers. Moisture, soil conditions, pest threats, and more can be identified and preventative steps taken. This decreases manual labor and reduces reaction time, giving a farmer

enhanced knowledge to make strategic decisions.

- Crop storage optimization — Sensors can be calibrated to monitor and even adjust temperature levels and humidity levels. This can optimize crop storage conditions, which makes harvested crops last longer.
- Livestock monitoring — IoT tech is also available for livestock monitoring and management. IoT enabled tags or collars can help owners maintain herd health. This is another instance of automation that alleviates manual or repetitious tasks, as well as providing early alerts for preventable problems.
- Logistics Traceability — IoT technology improves logistics by increasing efficiency and transparency throughout the supply chain, as well as providing immutable traceability. By reducing media breaks and improving the precision of tracking, IoT supports speed and accuracy with end-to-end tracking capabilities.

9 798889 517764

Printed by Libri Plureos GmbH in Hamburg, Germany